D1064996

The publisher gratefully acknowledges the generous support of the Classical Literature Endowment Fund of the University of California Press Foundation, which was established by a major gift from Joan Palevsky.

The Gnat and Other Minor Poems of Virgil

The Gnat and Other
Minor Poems of Virgil

TRANSLATED BY DAVID R. SLAVITT

Foreword by Gordon Williams

 University of California Press   Berkeley Los Angeles London

University of California Press, one of the most distinguished univer-
sity presses in the United States, enriches lives around the world by
advancing scholarship in the humanities, social sciences, and natural
sciences. Its activities are supported by the UC Press Foundation
and by philanthropic contributions from individuals and institu-
tions. For more information, visit www.ucpress.edu.

University of California Press
Berkeley and Los Angeles, California

University of California Press, Ltd.
London, England

Library of Congress Cataloging-in-Publication Data

Virgil.
    [Appendix Vergiliana. English]
    The gnat and other minor poems of Virgil / Virgil ; translated by
David R. Slavitt.
        p.   cm.
    A new translation of nine Latin poems attributed to Virgil.
    ISBN 978-0-520-26765-7 (cloth : alk. paper)
    1. Virgil—Translations into English. 2. Latin poetry—
Translations into English. I. Slavitt, David R., 1935– II. Title.
    PA6956.E5   2011
    871'.01—dc22   2010032663

Manufactured in the United States of America

19   18   17   16   15   14   13   12   11
10   9   8   7   6   5   4   3   2   1
The paper used in this publication meets the minimum requirements
of ANSI/NISO Z39.48-1992 (R 1997) (*Permanence of Paper*).

For Gordon Williams

In memoriam

Contents

Foreword

The only link that unites the medley of poems in The Virgilian Appendix is the fact that they were tossed together into one manuscript. Then the title Appendix Virgiliana was invented for this collection in the sixteenth century. The word "Appendix" asserts that these poems are an addendum to the three canonical works of Virgil *(Eclogues, Georgics, Aeneid)* that established for the Renaissance the ideal career of the poet.

In fact, not one of the poems in the Appendix can plausibly be attributed to Virgil. What needs emphasis in this context is that poetry was a major source of entertainment for educated Romans, recited on all possible occasions (for instance dinner parties) by aspiring artists—and few were the Romans who did not feel within themselves the urge of the Muse. Think of Cinna, who, when the mob went on a rampage of revenge after the murder of Julius Caesar, was seized by them. As told by Shakespeare (on the basis of an anecdote in Plutarch), he pleads: "I am Cinna the poet, I am Cinna the poet . . ." The mob replies: "Tear him for his bad verses, tear him for his bad verses." Or there is the great Cicero, of whose poetry sufficient has come down to us to reveal that he had not the faintest tinge of poetic sensibility.

Aspiring poets were often invited to the dinner parties of the wealthy to give recitations. Petronius creates a splendid burlesque of the practice in the episode known as The Dinner Party of Trimalchio. This Trimalchio was an immensely rich and vulgar freedman, imitating the social conventions of his betters as best he knew how.

All but three of the poems collected in the Appendix were most probably composed in the Julio-Claudian period that extended from the death of Augustus in AD 12 to the death of Nero in AD 68. They clearly display a knowledge not only of Virgil's canonical poems but also of the poetry of Ovid. These years were notorious for the extravagantly luxurious lifestyle of the wealthy, and this provided a comfortable and supportive ambience for varied poetic ambition.

Of course, any educated Roman could sense within himself the urge (and the ability) to compose poetry, but there was always the awkward problem of inspiration: What was there to write about? What was the focus of the Muse? There were routine solutions to this painful difficulty: one could always, for instance, compose a description of the spectacular Sicilian volcano Aetna, and indeed there is such a poem in the Appendix in 645 hexameters (it has wisely been omitted by David Slavitt from among his elegant translations).

Three of the poems in the Appendix are now recognized to have been composed by Ausonius (c. 310–393), a Christian from Bordeaux and a distinguished poet and orator (some of whose work Slavitt has translated before). These are "De institutione viri boni," "De rosis nascentibus," and "De est et non"; in the translation they are "The Good Man," "Budding Roses," and "Yes and No."

The culex "Mosquito" is particularly interesting because its poet made a deliberate attempt to deceive the reader. The poet addresses his purported patron as Octavi. This designates the man who later became Augustus, but the poet uses the name Octavius, which was later changed to Octavianus after testamentary adoption as his son by Julius Caesar. The poem, therefore, dates itself to before 44/43 BC, and what was regrettably missing, a poem written by a very young Virgil, is now happily supplied. Alas! This is a blatant impossibility since the culex displays clear knowledge of the *Aeneid* and especially of the Underworld as presented in Book 6.

Another poem, rather a good one, known as "Moretum," titled here "Pesto (*Moretum*)," describes, with the loving attention to detail of a dedicated cookbook author, the preparation of a ploughman's lunch with the assistance of his African slave girl. However, this poem shows clear knowledge of Ovid's work. Ovid died about AD 18, and so the poem cannot be by Virgil.

David Slavitt's selection picks out the best of these poems and gives us a welcome sense of the quality of the numerous minor poets in the Julio-Claudian period and later in his elegant translations.

Gordon Williams

Introduction

This mixed bag of poems was called the Virgilian Appendix by Josephus Justus Scaliger, the Dutch philologist and historian, in 1572. There had been a tradition of crediting Virgil with the writing of various of these poems, and Statius, Lucan, Martial, Quintilian, and Suetonius could all be cited (not always directly or convincingly) as authorities. Modern scholars have decided, however, that none of the poems is likely to have been Virgil's.

The effects of the misattribution have been equivocal. The advantage has been that the poems were preserved, Virgil's name having had a certain authority. (Even today, poetry editors look at the name first, and then at the poem.) The disadvantage is that modern readers somehow blame the poems for this mistake and seem to hold them responsible for being "fakes."

There is a difference, though, between a fake and a misattribution. The former is an intentional fraud on the part of the writer (or painter), while the latter is an error for which the writer and his poem cannot be held responsible. It is improbable that Scaliger was intentionally trying to mislead anyone or to profit in any way from his verdict. And it would be a shame if we were to dismiss these pieces, which are appealing, charming, and affable. If they were good enough to have been mistaken for the work of Virgil, that should count in their favor rather than the other way. Think of them, if you will, as a sheaf of anonymous poems, in which case they do not labor under so heavy a burden.

It seems wrong-headed to despise them as A. E. Housman did. He calls the authors of "The Gnat" and a couple of other pieces that I have omitted, "mediocre poets and worse; and the gods and men and booksellers whom they affronted by existing allotted them for transcription to worse than mediocre scribes." He says these poets were "stutterers; but what they stuttered and twaddled was Latin, not double-Dutch; and the great part of it is now double-Dutch, and Latin no more."

We love that kind of vitriol (as long as it isn't directed at us). It is not only amusing, but it offers us an excuse to ignore whatever work the critic may have been talking about. We have enough books to read, movies and plays to see, and paintings to look at as it is.

They are not all anonymous. It is more than likely that "Yes and No," "Budding Roses," and "The Good Man" were the work of Decimus Magnus Ausonius, who happens to be one of my favorite Latin poets. To start with, he is said to have lived outside Bordeaux at Chateau Ausonne, which makes a premier grand cru St. Emilion, one of the finest wines of the world. (He probably didn't live there, but this misattribution is decorative and honorific, especially if you ever had the good fortune to taste "his" wine.)

He was a *grammaticus* (instructor) and then a *rhetor* (professor) at the University of Bordeaux, and his family was politically well-connected. He could therefore afford to be playful, whimsical, and deeply unserious, all of which generally appeals to me. (His serious poem, *Mosella,* is a catalogue of all the fish that can be found in that river and a travelogue of the buildings and cities that one would see on a trip along that waterway. I find that less riveting.)

His "Nuptial Cento" is an extended prep-school-boy's prank, a pastiche of bits from Virgil snipped together to make an obscene epithalamion. In a shamelessly show-off exercise, I "translated" that a decade ago, using Shakespeare as my source text and covering more or less the same narrative ground in the same smoker atmosphere.[1] "The Commemorations of the Professors of Bordeaux," which is also in that volume, is an endearingly clubbable series of poems about teachers and colleagues he knew in the fourth century, some of them good, some of them less so, and one or two of them raffish or truly stupid.

The others? Who knows? Who actually cares? Good poems, even good minor poems, are worth keeping alive, and these bijoux should not be kept to graduate students and classics professors (who appreciate them all too seldom). "The Gnat," a miniature epic or epyllion, is an extravagant fable, the kind of performance that reminds us of La Fontaine or Avianus.[2] Or, to put it another way, it is a children's poem for grown-ups, and it deserves to be resuscitated.

"The Barmaid" is a conventional *carpe diem* poem, a sophisticated (but not too sophisticated) version of a saloon song. "Curses" is a grim amusement, to be compared to Ovid's "Ibis," a long, elaborate series of maledictions that finally reveal the powerlessness of the speaker. "Lydia" is the sad utterance of an exile remembering both the land and the woman he has lost, with the losses merging and reinforcing each other—as in Vladimir Nabokov's wonderfully moving first novel, *Mary.* The Priapus poems are spoken by the crude wooden phallus that farmers used to erect to protect their fields in a practice that elicits sniggers in schoolboys but which they come in later life to learn has a certain validity and meaning. "Pesto," which is how I translate "Moretum" is the account of a poor, simple farmer fixing his dinner, a country scene that I think of as appealing to city folks who yearn for something else, something more natural and "real" than the political and economic struggles of urban life. "Budding Roses" is a simple lyric that Robert Herrick may have had in mind when he wrote his similar poem. And "Yes and No" is a grammarian's interesting and perhaps self-mocking expostulation of the curious world view that his kind of study can lead to.

I have omitted "Ciris" in part because I don't like it all that much, but more important, because it doesn't easily migrate across time. It is rife with references, and the game was for the reader to recognize as many as he could (and then congratulate himself) or, failing that, to congratulate the poet for his extensive and arcane knowledge. There used to be quirky quizzes on the last page of the *Times Literary Supplement* that I always looked at, not in any way expecting to be able to answer more than one or two of the questions, but as a spiritual exercise—because they reminded me how much I didn't know and kept me humble. "Ciris" is like that. There would be a way of doing it with a great many footnotes, but that would be like doing riddles with the answer right there on the same page and defeat the purpose of the poem.

So, no "Ciris" and no "Aetna" either, the latter being a kind of scientific poem, what Lucretius would have written if he'd had less talent. It is an exercise in tedium, and I spare not only my readers but myself in leaving it out. Both of these are available in the Loeb Library editions, in the volume that has the second part of the Aeneid, in Latin with a prose translation *en face*.

Finally, I left out the "Catalepton," a potpourri of short pieces on assorted subjects, more or less like pieces from the Greek Anthology, but seldom up to that level. This was a tactical decision, because it seemed to me to make sense either to do them all or to omit them all. It also struck me that a few of them presented almost insoluble challenges.

For instance, VII reads:

Si licet, hoc sine fraude, Vari dulcissime dicam:
   "dispeream, nisi me perdidit iste Pothos:"
sin autem praecepta vetant me dicere, sane
   non dicam, set "me perdidit iste puer."

Obviously, it's a slight thing, a quip, really. More or less:

I beg pardon, Varius old pal, but
I'd say that that cute Pothos of yours slays me.
If the rules prohibit that, then of course I won't,
but still, that cute boy of yours slays me.

I hate it when the explanations are longer than the poems, but you have to know that Varius was a friend of Virgil's, and that the author of the epigram was pretending to be Virgil. You also have to know that *pothos* is the Greek word for "desire," which is coincidentally the name of the slave in the poem and also a common form of address from master to slave. What the poem is about, though, is that the use of the Greek word was considered pretentious and against the rules, and that in the second version of the phrase "Pothos" therefore becomes "boy," so that, while the rule is no longer broken, the same sentiment gets itself expressed. A big laugh? Well, maybe not, but the poem is, in its slight, snide way, mildly amusing—except that its joke is unreachable in twenty-first century English.

The remaining pieces are fine examples of Latin poetry of the Silver Age and later, and I am not alone in my admiration of them. Other poets have picked out one or another to turn into English poetry. Spenser did a breezy version of "The Gnat" in ottava rima, Cowper produced a pleasing rendition of the "Moretum" ("Pesto"), and Lamb did the three Priapus poems. But the poems, finally, speak for themselves. And *pace* Housman's dissatisfaction, they have pleased me enough so that I was happy to devote time to them. Come to think of it, that wouldn't have been an issue for Housman anyway, for he devoted much of his life to editing the texts of Manilius, a first century poet whose only work is the *Astronomica,* which he himself despised. (As do I.)

The only important issue is whether the reader feels that his or her time has been well or ill spent. Was it fun or not? In some measure, that may depend upon what your anticipation was before you began to read them. For some people, if they are honest, their first visit to Paris or Rome or London is disappointing, because their expectations were impossibly high and those great cities are difficult to get to know right away. On the other hand, a stop in, say, Ravenna, or Besançon, might be a delightful surprise because there were no preconceived notions that came in the luggage. That these are not really by Virgil allows for that kind of pleasant surprise.

NOTES

1. *Ausonius: Three Amusements,* David R. Slavitt, trans., University of Pennsylvania Press, 1998.

2. See *The Fables of Avianus,* David R. Slavitt, trans., Johns Hopkins University Press, 1993.

The Gnat and Other Minor Poems of Virgil

THE GNAT

My dear Octavius . . . But do I forget myself?
No, on the contrary, I remember, as you do, too,
those old days when we fooled around, just starting out,
each on his own path, but good friends then and now.
Back then, as baby spiders sometimes do, I made
the frail and tiny webs that you would not think could hold
any kind of prey. But how else can they begin?
Let me return to that playful making of miniatures
that can be, I think, endearing, and are able to sustain
more than one might suppose. A plot! The speeches of heroes,
allusions to gods and all the Muses' elaborate stagecraft.
The bass notes will come later, but for the moment let us
turn our attention to this, the narrative of a gnat.
Will critics carp? I defy them! Their views are of even less
weight than the gnat would claim. All they want is uplift
and sound ideas. The poet has other, more important
business he must transact—as you so well understand.
This may be a jeu d'esprit but it can claim your attention
because its inspiration comes from Phoebus Apollo,
the golden child of Zeus and Latona and source of my song.
Let him inspire me with riffs on his harp that sound
like Xanthus' babble coming down Mt. Chimaera's slopes
to pass the town of Arna. Or better yet, imagine
the Castalia's steady murmur high on Parnassus' ridge
between the two rocky cliffs that appear to be great horns.
There the Naiads dance, thronging about the god,
while Pales, the shepherds' goddess, blesses her devotees
with increase in their flocks and keeps the woodlands green.

Tend those who tend the beasts, that I may roam the glades
taking whatever I can of their cool green inspiration.

And you, my dear Octavius, you also deign to bless
my efforts and to inspire, by your manifest merit,
the confidence I need for any such undertaking.
My lines will not sound the clangor of battle and bloody fighting,
and I shall not speak of war. The gigantomachy at Phlegra
that crimsoned the brown duff with the blood of the dying giants
is not what I have in mind. The Lapiths' brawl with the Centaurs
demands a recklessness that both you and I might question.
The Persian assault upon Athens with Xerxes' digging a channel
through Athos' foothills, and then later their ruinous flight
would make for the kind of splendid piece one dreams of writing,
but not until the wisdom—whatever there is—of age
supports the prosodist's craft with its bittersweet understanding.
Let's put that off a little, when the thirst for fame may prompt
ambitious undertakings for you of course, but for me,
too, in my own way. These are the tender shoots
of the flowers of early spring when Phoebus comes to wake
the long-slumbering earth with the warmth of his attention.
Let us wander barefoot as the young know how to do
on the almost velvety greensward. The holy youth I knew
was not yet burned by fame that waits upon you now
but I suspect you knew that it would one day arrive
as you know now that your place in heaven's abode is secure
from which your glistening presence will pour its blessings down
to inspire men and let them know of the joys of the good.

The sun has just risen up from its underground lair to shine
in the eastern sky and scatter its gift of golden rays,

and Aurora yet again has set the Darkness to flight
when a herdsman comes on the scene, driving his goats before him
and climbing the mountainside on his way to the happy pastures
where the grass still wet with the dew covers the gentle slopes.
The animals wander here and there, as if they have
a program they follow, but, no, it's just a series of promptings
of this attractive thicket, that delightful knoll,
and they crop the grass and nibble, composing as they do so
a picture of contentment for which we, in the city,
sometimes feel a yearning. Look at the rocky hollows,
the vines, the trailing arbutus, the delicate weeping willow
where the animals amble or sometimes, for no apparent reason,
caper and run, or then, as arbitrarily, rest.
Why should it be so pleasing to watch as a nanny goat stretches
her neck to take the delicate new leaves of the alder
that overhangs the stream, with no idea whatever
of the landscape she's in that sets her utter concentration
into a context of ease, tranquility, and peace?
          Which of us has never thought of becoming a herdsman
and accepting the invitation of that pastoral scene? We dream
of power and wealth, of achievement, and are taught to feel disdain
for the poor man's bare-bones existence. But who in the city can claim
the happiness goatherds must feel at moments and settings like this?
The luxuries around us weigh us down with cares
as they whet our appetites for ever greater indulgence
so that our hearts are never at rest but always questing
to satisfy those whims that swirl around in our heads.
How fine to have our fleeces vividly double-dyed
in bright Assyrian colors, but can this satisfy?

Not all of Attalus' booty or gold-leaf glints from the ceiling
can sate the greedy soul, relentless in its craving.
Handsome paintings, gaudy jewels, the golden goblets
of an Alcon or a Boethus cannot quench such thirst
that burns as if from a fever. But there in that pleasant meadow
with a heart that is free from guile, the herdsman lies down happy,
stretched on emerald grass highlighted with dewdrops
where spring puts pastel accents of blossoms wherever he looks.
He stretches out his hand to pluck a reed from the river
and with it makes simple music, sweeter than our soirées
can ever provide in a salon abuzz with envy and hate.
This is the kind of playing Tmolus judged and enjoyed,
and sometimes the goats pause, look up from their grass and stare,
pleased at the sound they take to be that of some nearby bird.
With leaves and vines, goat milk, spring water, fruits and flowers
and all the gifts of Pales nourishing flesh and spirit,
where in his full heart can greed find a place to invade?

There must have been, long ago, a happier time, a golden
or silver age when all mankind lived in this manner,
free of the goads of greed, or war, or the fear of war,
the pitched battles on land, or the conflicts of fleets at sea,
in which men fight with men in the hope of plunder to pile
on the altars of cruel gods. His god is gentle and kind
with his rude images hacked in wood with a pruning knife.
Priapus does not require impressive marble figures
but only these frank gestures of the country people's devotion
and thanks for the benefits they see everywhere around them
in the green fields so richly speckled with colorful flowers.
Panchaea, that fabulous island in the Erythrean sea,

cannot boast of richer, more subtle perfumes than those
that waft in the gentle breeze with their ever-changing scents.
When his days of gratification have faded away with the sunlight,
his sleep is undisturbed by the kinds of dreams that torment us
with their burdens of fears and regrets. There is no silken pillow
that offers our heads the sweet repose of his contentment
as his weary body lolls in the sweetness of honest fatigue.
O flocks and herds! O Pans! O Tempe's idyllic valley
where the beautiful Hamadryads dwell in the trees! The herdsmen
have all this and rejoice, and each competes with his brothers
in songs of thanks and praise to the deities of his world
in the strains that Hesiod took for himself to descant upon
in *Works and Days,* his splendid poem of country life.

       These are the satisfactions the shepherd enjoys as he leans
on his crook and daydreams (but only of more and more of the same)
or plays upon his Syrinx tunes or just random notes
as the sun climbs heaven's vault and pours down dazzling rays
that change their angle with every passing hour from dawn
through high noon until dusk. Then does the herdsman gather
his flock together as shadows lower upon the hillsides.
In one of those sheltered places he likes for the night, Diana
once saw Agave, daughter of Cadmus and Harmonia,
murder her own son, staining her wicked hands
with Pentheus' blood. When Bacchus' frenzy abated at last,
she ran away and hid from him in a cave like this one.
In a place like this did Pan and the Satyrs romp with Dryad
and Naiad girls, dancing the merry night away.
We know about Orpheus' song and how it made the Hebrus'
waters pause in their flow, but that was a brief interruption,

lasting much less long than the dancing out in the woods
that made Diana pause to watch and share their delight.
We know these tales of course and tell them to one another
here in the city, but there, in the countryside Diana
is so much loved, one can feel that she may have excused herself
for only a moment and therefore may return in the next.
It is the city dweller's yearning that makes her presence
so palpable as we think of her radiating her joys
among the whispering leaves and refreshing shade that the weary
recognize as blessings. The towering plane trees sway
over the lotus—wicked for what it did to Ulysses'
comrades, holding them captive in indolence and *douceur*.
The poplars, of course, are Phaëthon's sisters, the Heliads,
transformed in their fall from the blazing car to earth where they lift
their slender arms toward heaven, veiled in the white of mourning.
And Phyllis is there, who turned at her death to an almond tree,
the fruit of which is as bitter as the tears the young girl shed
for Demophoön after he left Thrace and forgot
all about her (a story that girls even today
weep to hear). And the oak trees, the kind we find at Dodona,
where vatic ladies chant their hints about what is to come,
used to provide us with food before the gifts of Ceres
improved and refined our lives, as Triptolemus traveled the earth
teaching men to plant, tend, and then harvest wheat.
And there in the woods are the shaggy pines the planks of which
were used to build the *Argo*—and those lofty trees aspire
to touch the starry skies where the Argonauts' constellations
revolve through the changing seasons. And look, there, at the ilex,
the sad cypress, the umbrous beeches, and see the ivies

constraining the poplars' arms lest, for their brother's sake,
they smite themselves with blows. The ivy climbs their branches
and dapples their golden clusters with accents of deepest green.
But have I mentioned the myrtle, the tree into which Myrsine,
Venus' priestess, was changed? (She had offended the goddess
who loved her nevertheless and made her tree evergreen.)
      Among these various trees, the birds light on the branches
to sing their different songs. Beneath them the trickle of water
flowing over the rocks murmurs of calm and peace.
In answer to those birds a comic chorus of frogs
responds with querulous croaks from the homes they make in the muck,
and adding their note, the cicadas whirr in the heat of the day
that all of nature seems to have joined together to praise.
      That's the scene, except for the sheep that are lying here
and there, resting and chewing their cud, as the random breezes
tousle their fleeces. The shepherd also decides to lie down,
weary with heat and happy to sojourn in his dream world
and drift off into a sleep in which his dreams will be
redundant. What possible reason could he have at a time and place
as idyllic as that for any worries or vivid fears?
This, you will have realized, is always a risky question,
the asking of which is often enough to invite disaster.
That may have been the reason—or there may have been none whatever—
for Fortune to decide that his sense of contentment and safety
was too much for her to allow, and in its habitual course
an enormous speckled serpent made its way to seek
shelter from the heat and perhaps a drink from the pond.
We can see the flickering tongue emerge from its fetid mouth
as it corkscrews along at a fair clip on its scaly coils.

Its expression seems to be one of absolute rage, unless
it is only the glowing eyes that give one such an impression.
It lifts its head and glances this way and that in spite;
the purple scales of its neck glisten as if they were armor;
and the crest on its head comports well with that martial effect.
It surveys the ground or say that it reconnoiters. It sees
the shepherd blocking its way. It narrows its yellow eyes
and continues on the course that is, at least for the moment,
obstructed by this large being stretched out on the ground.
The snake and its kind do not put up with such frustrations
but seize and crush to death whatever impedes their progress.
It's how they are wired perhaps, but no other possible answers
present themselves to the serpent. It performs as Nature has taught it,
hissing in wrath and showing its fangs (this often suffices
to solve its difficulties, for obstacles flee if they can).
It coils itself and rears in preparation for striking,
and the hideous mouth yawns in a minatory display.
The shepherd, as we remember, is lost to the world and cannot
have any idea of the terrible danger closing upon him.
And then? And then what happens? One of Nature's nurslings
arrives in time to warn him, stinging his eyelid to rouse him
and warn him that death impends. It has picked a tender place
either by chance or else, if this is a fable, then knowing
that this is the quickest way to wake him up, and time,
as they often say in the courtrooms, is of the essence. The eye
hurts and the shepherd wakes and strikes the little gnat dead!
What sacrifice to lay down one's life for another creature,
but the poor gnat has been crushed and become a tiny smudge
on the shepherd's weathered face. It's then that he sees the serpent

coiled quite close and looking angry and ready to strike.
He does not stop to think but grabs a nearby bough
from one of the trees and, inspired, uses the branch as a cudgel
beating upon the serpent again and again in a frenzy
one would not have supposed him able to summon up
from his frail and aged frame. The strength and also the courage
are those of a younger man with a martial disposition.
He smashes the snake on its crest and crushes the oval skull.
How can this happen? Remember he had just woken up
a moment ago and had no time to experience fears
that otherwise would have attended such heroic exertions.
But now that the snake is dispatched, he feels the clammy terror
seize his skinny limbs. He can hardly breathe or stand.
The sense of his danger comes belatedly and he
can't quite believe that he is alive and the snake is dead
there on the ground before him, crushed, and by his efforts.
His knees wobble. He sinks back to the ground and sits there
feeling no pride at all but the terror still, and amazement.
          Erebus' wife, Night, is now urging her steeds
across the sky. Ascending from behind golden Mt. Oeta
the evening star is advancing. The shepherd pens his sheep
and after this eventful day lies down to rest
his utterly exhausted body in healing repose.
He drifts off and his limbs relax and then his mind
lets go of the outer world, but into its inviting
arena comes the minuscule ghost of the poor gnat
to inveigh against injustice and complain of ingratitude:
"Is this how I am repaid for my concern and aid
that saved your life? Aware of the risk to my own safety,

I roused you nevertheless, and look at me now—I roam
through the emptiness of space, while you stretch out to sleep,
having been snatched from the very lip of a yawning grave
and an agonizing death. My spirit is on its way
across the waters of Lethe in Charon's dismal skiff.
The ferryman's eyes brighten as if they were flames of torches
at a temple at festival time. Tisiphone brandishes whips
and Cerberus barks from all three mouths while hideous snakes
writhe around his necks and his eyes glow red as blood.
And do you feel gratitude? Do you even remember me?
Does Virtue go unrewarded? Is Goodness held up to contempt
and ridicule? Is Justice altogether forgotten?
The pieties that religion used to nurture have all
fallen in desuetude. The bases of civilization
are fictions that have life only if men believe.
I saw my duty and I performed it, giving no thought
to what the cost might be. I accept that death I risked—
but let there be a grateful heart that knows what I did
and let there be at least some small reciprocal gesture.
I wander these pathless infernal regions as dark as those
in which the Cimmerians dwell, and all around me is torture
for those who deserve to suffer. Otus and Ephialtes,
Neptune's twins, are here, who tried to mount the sky.
Tityus writhes, who offered to do Latona violence,
and the vulture tears at his liver. These are ghastly scenes
from which I turn away, but then, in another direction,
I see poor Tantalus' desperate efforts to slake his thirst
and satisfy his hunger. Sisyphus worries his boulder
endlessly up that hill. The Danaids scurry in pointless

labor carrying leaky vessels of water hither
and thither for their crimes. Medea is here of course,
and Philomela and Procne, with Tereus overhead
calling out in his hoopoe cry for *Itys, Itys* . . .
But what could be my connection with any of them and their crimes?
Or by what disproportion do I find myself in the same
venue as Polynices and Eteocles his brother,
both of their hands still stained with one another's blood?
It is necessary that I attempt to swim across
Elysium's wide waters. Persephone there urges
the heroine women to hold forth their unpropitious torches.
Alcestis is there having saved her husband Admetus from death
(much as I saved you, except that we weren't married).
Penelope is there, the glory of womankind,
and behind her as if in a diorama the many suitors
are disposed in various postures of sudden death with arrows
protruding from their lifeless bodies in every direction.
Eurydice too in those precincts of special virtue mourns
Orpheus' backward look that cost her that second chance
at life in the upper world where the light of the sun shines.
Whoever thinks that Cerberus cannot be stilled or that Dis
and its stern and implacable judges can never be moved to tears
rehearses their sad story with its faint flicker of hope.
He tells himself how Orpheus enchanted the rivers and trees
that were touched by his song and either stopped in their rocky beds
or contrived to move their deepest roots to come closer to listen.
High in the starry sky, the moon's matched pair of horses
paused to hear his lyre, the power of which possessed
Persephone too, the bride of the Lord of the Underworld,

so that she, of her own free will, gave Eurydice up,
or at least she tried. But Death, who takes us all in the end,
snared Eurydice back, although she'd done nothing wrong.
Orpheus raised her hopes and then, by his want of faith,
dashed them. (But I am afraid that art will often do that,
with its vision of a better world we can never reach.)
Her existence is now more painful than before her lover descended
and tried and failed to retrieve her. Across from that heroine band
is a group of deserving heroes. Both of Aeacus' sons
are there—they are Telamon and Peleus—secure
in their places among the blest, their father being a judge
in the underworld. (Peleus, you will remember, married
Thetis; Telamon's wife was Periboea.) The two
couples' sons were Achilles and Ajax, from whose exploits
one could recount the entire Trojan war that stained
the Xanthus and Simois red with the blood of men.
        "Along the shores of Sigaeum, men from the Troad came
to slaughter the Greeks and attempt to burn their long black ships,
inspired by Hector's rage and by having walked the slopes
of Ida, which fills the hearts of all who ascend it with ire.
Its trees became firebrands that its devotees waved aloft
and used to set ships aflame. The smoke brought tears to the eyes
of even the bravest Achaians. Telemonian Ajax
came out to offer combat to Hector himself, the chief
defender of Troy. Just as in springtime when rivers roar
with sudden snowmelt and thunder down on plains below
to devastate farmers' fields, so from the heights of Troy
did spears and flaming arrows rain down on Greek ships,

but unlike the grain in the fields, they fought back with their swords
to repel the savage assault and maintain themselves on their beach-head.
      "It was cheering to Telamon and Peleus to see
the Achaians triumph when Hector was killed and his body was dragged
around the walls, but their happiness turned abruptly to woe
when Paris slew Achilles, and the wily Ulysses drove
Ajax raving mad. Down here, they avoid each other,
and Ulysses eyes never meet Telamon's outraged glare.
That proud Ithacan king, who murdered Rhesus of Strymon
(whom oracles had said would be the savior of Troy),
exposed Dolon, the spy, and stole the Trojan's statue
that was said to keep their city safe from any attack,
now cowers in fear of the great anger of the Cicones
and the Laestrygonians too. Scylla, with her hounds,
menaces him and he cringes; the Cyclops hates his guts;
and Charybdis contorts her face in withering disdain.
      "Here too is Atreus' son, scion of Tantalus' house,
under whose rule the Greeks laid waste the Trojan plain
for which they paid a heavy penance as their ships
were wrecked off the coast of Euboea. Fortune contrives to punish
those who have risen too high, as Nemesis comes to correct
the sins of pride. The returning ships had made good progress
on a calm sea with following winds and Nereids guiding
their helmsmen to home port, but then, through chance or fate,
the sky changed, and the winds whipped around, and the sea
was churned into a maelstrom that threatened to wash the welkin
of high heaven. The heavily laden vessels wallowed
and foundered in the tempest. The triumphant Greeks were reduced

to terror and then despair as first one, then another
craft crashed upon rocks at Caphereus or else
destroyed itself at the base of the cliffs of Euboea, and booty
plundered from the Phrygian treasuries and their temples
sank to the bottom or else drifted as flotsam toward shore.

   "Here are Romans, too, the brave and glorious heroes
one might expect to find—the Fabii, of course,
and the Decii; Horatius (the one from the famous bridge);
and Camillus, who came back from an unjust exile to save us
from the siege of the Gauls; and Curtius, too, who flung himself
into the depths of the cavern that opened up and demanded
the city's greatest treasure (without which it would destroy us).
Musius, who endured the flames until they consumed
his right hand (and Porsenna was terrified and yielded),
is present as is the frugal Curius who preferred
his earthen pots to the gold and silver ones the Samnites
offered him as a bribe. Caecilius is here
 who gave his eyes, and Regulus and the Scipios, who reduced
Carthage to random thickets in a desolate wasteland.

   "Let them all flourish and thrive in their renown. Those precincts
in which the elect consort are not for the likes of me,
and I must go on, I fear, to oblivion's shadowy pools
and the waters of Phlegathon to which Minos consigns
those who were not heroes. To the fiends with scourges I plead
my sorry case, but you do not come to bear witness.
My story is unsupported and appears to be self-serving,
and what judge will believe the claim I put before him?
I am a mere gnat, but I shall miss the springtime,
the green groves of the forest, the sweet smells of the meadows.

My complaint may seem small—like me—but what I did
I did for you. And can you allow the random breezes
to disperse my posthumous words and obliterate the truth?"
That was all he had to say. Then with a small
whine that gnats produce when they fly he disappeared.
         The shepherd woke up, not right away but soon enough
so he could remember his dream. Or was it a visitation?
His heart was flooded with sorrow and bitter chagrin. He arose
and returned to that glade where he started to dig in the grassy sod,
marking out a circle on which he could set the stones
fashioned from polished marble. This monument he bedecked
with myrtle from Sparta, acanthus, crimson roses, and violets.
He put in Cilician saffron, and laurel, Apollo's plant.
Oleander and lilies, and rosemary (for its perfume)
he placed in an artful design, with juniper accents (the berries
have a smell that resembles frankincense). And ivy
with its clusters of pale berries among its shiny leaves.
Amaranth, bumastus, perennial laurestine,
and Narcissus' pretty flowers decorated the mound.
Upon its face he put a plaque with an epitaph:
O GNAT, YOUR BODY WAS TINY, BUT YOUR HEART AND COURAGE
    WERE HUGE.
A GRATEFUL SHEPHERD PAYS YOU THIS TRIBUTE FOR SAVING
    HIS LIFE.

THE BARMAID

The Syrian barmaid gets up to dance. Her hair
is bound in a Greek bandanna and she sways
to the sizzle of a tambourine. Her bare
thighs flash through her skirt as the fiddle plays
and she winks at us and leers. In the smoky air
she sings a little song. This is what it says:

"Why would you think of leaving? It's dusty out there
and hot as blazes. Better to stay where you are,
sipping those cool drinks that we prepare
and hearing the pretty girls who strum a guitar.
Look, there are pots of flowers everywhere.
What better have you to do than hang out in a bar?

"Those pastoral figures playing on pipes of Pan
as they lay in the grass . . . Learn from their example.
We've just opened a new jar of wine and we can
provide for you from our excellent and ample
supply to soothe the troubles of any man.
We also have hors d'oeuvres for you to sample.

"In the fountain water plashes with a sound
that soothes, and delicate rose and saffron scents
suggest an idyllic glade. You may be bound
on some important errand, but what difference
if you do it tomorrow? Try not to let the hound
of conscience growl too loudly and harry you hence.

"Consider instead those plums or the little cheeses
in the osier basket. And chestnuts! And fresh red
apples! It is an array that always pleases.

A glass of wine? Some cheddar? A bit of bread?
How can you deny yourself? What eases
the body and spirit is good, as the poets have said.

"On that wall, there are cucumbers to slice
and eat with a touch of salt perhaps on the plate.
Priapus, the god of the house, offers advice
on what life is about—although that great
member he has might frighten more than entice
women, except for the most degenerate.

"The god, you may recall, tried once to attack
Vesta,[1] but a donkey's random bray
alerted her, and the goddess, thinking back
to how the assault was averted on that day,
is fond of donkeys. Yours, out in the shack,
is resting. For Vesta's sake, allow him to stay.

"Have another glass of wine, or a beaker,
and lie back, to enjoy a girl's caress
of your face and hair. What in the world could be bleaker
than ignoring all the flowers but those that will dress
your ungrateful ashes. Does your resolve grow weaker?
Do you begin to laugh at your seriousness?

"Never mind tomorrow. In my ear
Death whispers: 'Live! I'm coming. I am here!' "

NOTES

The "Copa" is ascribed to Virgil, almost certainly incorrectly, by Charisius and Priscian. It is about one of those tavern/brothels that Suetonius mentions as being common in Ostia and the bay of Baiae.

1. Ovid tells the story in *Fasti* vi, 319–349.

CURSES

Battarus, my friend, let us sing together our sad swan-song
    in grief and rage that our homes have been taken from us,
    and the lands we loved and lived on are ours no longer.
Sooner shall kids attack the slavering wolves, or calves
    harry the lions from hillsides; sooner shall dolphins flee
    the schools of fish in the sea, or eagles fly from doves;
sooner shall chaos come back to jumble up creation
    than my shepherd's reed shall be silenced, or my heart
    stop telling of Lycurgus' wicked depredations,
    calling out to the woods and the mountainsides in complaint.

May Sicily's happy valleys and fertile fields deny you
        the pleasures of increase. May the hills begrudge you pasture;
        the orchards, fruit; the vines, grapes; the trees, leaves.
        May all the familiar streams dry up in their rocky beds.

O Battarus, my friend, let it be this and more!

Let weeds grow in your fields to crowd out Ceres' gifts
        and may the green grasslands turn the pale yellow of death.
        May apples never ripen and fall and from their sickened branches.
But let not the notes of my angry singing fade away.
        May the delicate flowers of springtime wither away in the heat
        that comes untimely to kill them. Let the breezes depart
        to leave only blasting heat and poisons that float in the air.
        May your eyes and nose and ears yearn for anything sweet.

O Battarus, my friend, let it be this and more!

I used to wander among the tall trees with my flute
 and the wind now and then rustled the leaves that were high above me.
 But no more, Battarus, no more. I am gone, and the trees
 may also be gone as that rough soldier's impious hand
 takes an ax to fell them for carpenter's timber and fuel.

With those bosky shadows laid waste, and the sad scars of the stumps
 marking for those who know the land where the ruined
 grove once stood, the wretched place will be fertile ground
 for curses and imprecations. Let Lycurgus burn
 in the fierce fires of hell, to fuel Jupiter's ire.

These were his trees, his woods that this man turns to ashes.
 Let the North Wind come to blast his sorry life;
 Let the East Wind come, driving black clouds before it.
 Let the Southwest Wind pour bitter rain upon your head.

When you start to burn out the stumps may the fire spread to your vineyard,
 consume the grape vines and then, whipped by the wind, devour
 whatever poor crop you have managed to coax from the grudging field.
 Let the sparks spread fire up to your boundary line
 and everything within, houses and outbuildings,
 all be reduced to black and smoldering acrid ash.

O Battarus, friend, let it be this and more!

Waves that beat at the rocks of the shoreline in their relentless
　　　anger and the restless winds that cross overhead
　　　as if looking for something, hear me, angry as you.
　　　Let Neptune drive the water landward to flood his fields
　　　with deathly salt and sand. Let Vulcan burst forth in flames
　　　to make a second Libyan desert or sandbank.

O Battarus, friend, let it be this and more!

There are fierce beasts in those depths, many horrid monsters.
　　　May Neptune drive them up the beaches to come for you,
　　　herding them with his trident and goading them ever onward.
　　　Let the waves on which they ride swallow the ashes
　　　left by the fires that raged to destroy all that you seized,
　　　and let men come to stare at the signal devastation
　　　and acknowledge among themselves that this was what you deserved.
　　　And let them remember me and think of my malediction.

If Neptune does not hear us or grant our fervent wish,
　　　then go and plead with the streams that always loved you, Battarus.
　　　I have done my worst, but join me in these efforts
　　　and let not the judges of Hades fail to hear our complaint.

Raise up the streams to come to inundate his holdings
　　　and destroy the farm to save it and keep it from vagabonds.

O Battarus, friend, let it be this and more!

Let marshes spring forth and swamps. Where once we harvested wheat
let him gather cattails and listen to croaking frogs.
These curses that break my heart are the prayers of the farm itself.

Let foreigners come to fish in shallow lakes that stand
in the place of fertile fields that are, like us, in exile
and hating those who have come to arrogate for themselves
what they never loved or deserved, not husbandmen but rapists.

Discord is an evil god, the author of war
and woe, and from Discord's bloody hands he received what was
my father's and mine as plunder—but not from the enemy's wealth.
Here Roman loots from Roman, and I stand on this hillock
looking my last at what my eyes always took for granted.

From here I shall pass into woodland and then from the hills I shall turn
for the last glimpse of the place that ought to be my place.
And only the goats descending from grazing higher up
will hear my groans that they will interpret—correctly—as bleating.
Priapus, guard them well and look after them. I cannot.

One last strain Battarus, friend, and then no more!

We have long been good companions and now we are bound forever,
sharing as we now do the memories of our youth,
for the countryside we wandered is utterly gone except
that the two of us remember, and thus can confirm for each other
what we had and, now and again, share its ghostly presence.

LYDIA

I remember those meadows and fields where Lydia still
wanders, remembering me, and sighing in sadness
for our lost love. They make each other vivid,
as my yearnings for her and for them conflate, and I hear
her humming the songs she once crooned into my ear.
        I remember those fields . . . I become those fields and feel
the imprint of her pretty bare feet as she crosses
that sloping hill to reach the vineyard and pluck
a grape or two, still green, to pucker her mouth.
Or among the meadow's flowers she may lie down
imprinting the grass with her body as she recalls
those moments of our love that, like the petals
of cut blossoms, are fading before our eyes.
If only I were there, the woods would rejoice,
and the meadows would preen, the twittering birds would hush,
and the babbling brook pause in its bed to listen
to my songs of a sadness as poignant as any prayer.
        I envy you, meadows and fields, possessing now
her whom I loved and was my delight. Far away
my very limbs diminish as grieving saps
my strength and my body cools like that of a patient
breathing his last as he approaches his death.
My darling is no longer by my side, and no one
on earth is as clever as she or nearly as lovely.
I only wonder that Jove, at home in the heights,
never noticed that here on earth was a greater
prize than Europa or Danaë in her tower.

Everywhere I look, Nature calls out
to mock me and insult me. No bull on his hill
lows in lust without some heifer responding
from her stall in the warm barn to his loud complaint.
The Billy goat is blessed as he bounds over the rocks
and climbs the mountainsides with his happy mate
with whom he delights to father his many kids.
This is the business and pleasure of males of every
species, and sooner or later for their laments
is a happy ending—and also a new beginning.
Only for men is Nature so grudging and cruel,
allowing only our grief to be bitter and endless.

      Look up some night at a starry sky and think
how the moon, between her cycles, has gone to Latmos
to visit her dear Endymion yet again.
Dear moon, you know the grief of separation
from your beloved. Pity one who grieves.
Or Pan, give ear to my complaint. Your Sirynx
is always with you, her mourning notes your own.
How many gods have yearned as I yearn now?
That golden age may be past, but the pains persist
in us who are less well equipped to bear them,
weaker, the playthings of Time, and our brief moments
are all we have. Look down with understanding
and do what you can to help us. You may not raise me
up to the stars—as Dionysus promoted
Ariadne to shine with her bright corona—

but show me mercy, knowing how much meaner
and briefer the lives of human beings must be.
                    What crime have I committed that my death
is justified as a penalty? I have not
sullied her chastity or stolen Love's
sweet satisfactions. Do not make me regret
my innocence and hers by making me pay
for that sweet crime I never perpetrated.
                    I think of those bold gods and those defiant
goddesses who seized for themselves what right
could never have claimed: Jupiter, even Juno
consorted with whomever they desired;
Venus lay with Adonis on the splendid grass,
decking his neck with flowers and with her arms;
I think of how she abandoned Vulcan, her husband,
to cavort as she did with handsome, naughty Mars;
or Aurora who left her aged Tithonus to blush for shame
and love of Orion. These are heaven's examples,
and the men and women who lived in the golden age
conducted themselves with almost the same bravura.
                    I lack their luck, their courage, their shameless strength.
Nature was more indulgent then, but I
was born too late. Our race is wretched. The Fates
now trifle with us, play havoc with our hearts,
and what remains of us is ashamed. We cannot,
as we pass in the road, look in each other's eyes.

PRIAPUS POEMS

I

In the springtime, roses all over me. Just lovely!
In summer, they deck me with sheaves of wheat. Nice!
In the autumn, they offer me various kinds of fruit.
But winter? It's cold, and I fear that the rude bumpkins
will steal my wooden figures and use them for fuel.

II

Here I am, traveler, hacked out of poplar wood,
guarding this little field and the farmer's cottage,
and looking after his kitchen garden—to protect them
and ward away the wicked hands of thieves.

In the spring, they deck me in flowers; in summer, wheat;
in the fall, grapes; in the winter, freezing olives.
From that pasture there, where the nanny-goat's udders swell,
they bring the milk to market and fatted lambs
to come back home with money. The young calf,
its mother's lowing echoing in its ears,
pours forth its bright blood on the altars of gods.

I warn you, then, revere this powerful god
and keep your hands to yourself. I tell you this
for your own good. Look at my huge prick
stiff for you. And what can it do to you?
It can warn you of the farmer who's on his way
with a cudgel of about this size and shape.
It's no mere metaphor: you can bugger off
or wait here and be buggered. It's up to you.

III

Priapus here. You fellows know who I am,
the old god of fertility. My image here,
chopped into shape with an axe, may not qualify
as a work of art, but I do my fucking job,
and the man who lives in this hut with his teen-aged son
is making out okay. They honor me,
weeding the brambles out of my little patch here
or bringing me small gifts to show that they're grateful.
They do the garlands, the sheaves of wheat, the fruit—
melons and fresh ripe apples and clusters of grapes.
Once a year, I get the blood of a goat,
and for this I do my sentry service for them.
I speak softly and carry a big dick,
looking after their orchard, vineyard, and fields.

So fuck off, boyos. Show me a little reverence.
There's a guy nearby who's richer than these paisans
and lacks respect for his Priapus. Go,
take what you can from him. He's just down the road.

IV

What's all this? The god is in a snit!
It's late at night and there's a pretty boy
cuddling in my arms and I'm left limp,
my penis perversely passionless and ignoring
any attempt to rouse its sleepy head.

What you have always preferred, Priapus, is standing
on guard in a grove of trees with garlands of vine leaves
decking your head and your big tool painted crimson.
We've offered you fresh-cut flowers and frightened the crows
and daws that would dare to peck your at sacred figure.
And this is how you behave? Nothing will get you
nothing. Abandoned, I will abandon you.
I'll knock you down and let you rot in the fields,
to lose your bright color and let the dogs
worry at you and befoul your wooden skin.

And you, my lazy penis, shrivel in shame,
a display of anti-priapism (whatever
one wants to call it). You're only good for pissing,
No pretty boy will flick you, stroke you, or squeeze
his smooth butt down on you; no pretty girl
will welcome you to her thighs. What you now deserve
is some old crone, a superannuated
slut with a slit that's dusty and hung with cobwebs—
the kind of woman who, in your good old days,
would have caused better tools than you to shrink in dismay.

But she with disgusting efficiency will jerk you
silly so that you're eager to enter in
to that monstrous cave of hers where stagnant pools
of the vintage jism of countless men congeal.

You like that, you little prick? You pathetic pizzle?
You've won this time, sleeping when you should have been
on duty. Next time, perhaps you'll redeem yourself.
You'll hear his footsteps in the hall and rouse
yourself, rigid with eagerness. Your desire
will make you a stiff ramrod, larger and larger
until the playful and ever gracious Venus
blesses you with a cataclysmic discharge.

PESTO *(MORETUM)*

It's still dark, but the night is almost over
and here and there the roosters confirm one another
announcing the break of day they have not yet
seen but somehow can feel is coming soon.
Simulus hears them and drags his weary bones
up from the rude pallet on which he has slept,
gropes his way through the dark to the hearth, and finds
at the heart of a burnt-out log a still-live coal
upon which he gently blows to waken the sluggish
flame. He takes a needle and pulls forth
the wick from his clay lamp to take the fire
and burn on its own. Guarding the flickering light
he goes to his larder and with his key unlocks
the plank door. There, from the pile of grain
he fills his measuring can for his day's ration.
        Now he goes out to the mill and on the shelf
he's got up on the wall, he puts his lamp.
He takes the tail of his shirt and he sweeps the upper
and lower millstones free of dust and grit.
With his left hand he pours the measured grain
into the mill and with his right turns
the handle that drives the wheel and does the work
of grinding the kernels into the coarse flour
that's the point of the exercise. It's a strenuous job
and sometimes he changes hands to let the right
rest while the left performs for a while to produce
the laborious circles. He does this every day
and it's tedious, boring work. He sings to himself
the strains of a barely recognizable tune,

which he interrupts to shout to Scybale to rouse her.
(She is his African servant, kinky-haired,
a bit flat-footed, black as coal, but always
smiling and showing a row of bright white teeth.)
When she hears him call from the mill she puts more fuel
onto the fire and fetches a kettle of water
she hangs on its hook over the flame to heat.
        Simulus, meanwhile, has come to the end
of this part of the job and pours out the ground grain
into a fine sieve he shakes back and forth
to let the flour go through but keep the black
husks on the upper side. The flour he spreads
on a table he's got in the kitchen near the hearth.
Now he pours some of the warm water
onto the flour that he packs together and kneads
to form larger and larger lumps of dough
to which he adds a little salt, or maybe
a little more of the water. He judges by feel
knowing what its consistency should be,
and he lets his fingers do the thinking for him.
When he's satisfied, he uses his open palms
to spread the dough into a rounded loaf
that he scores in a way to make four equal parts.
This he puts into the hearth in a place Scybale
has cleared for him and he rearranges the burning
sticks of the fire so that they're close but not
touching the bread that he wants to bake but not burn.
Now he has to turn his attention to what

will go with the bread. He doesn't have sides of bacon
hanging up in a smokehouse. He's not a rich man.
He does have a cheese suspended on a string
and near it a fair sized bunch of dried dill weed.
He does what he often does and goes out to his garden,
a small plot, set off by a row of reeds
that serve as a kind of fence. There he grows
various herbs, some for his own use,
and some to sell to richer men in the region.
It costs him nothing to do this. Whenever rain
or a holiday keeps him from going out to the fields,
he tends his kitchen garden, planting or weeding,
watering when the ground is dry, or thinning
the plants when they seem to crowd each other. He has
cabbages, beets with their leafy arms outspread,
sorrel, mallows, yellow elecampane
(its roots are good in ointments), as well as skirret
(or water parsnip: its roots are spongy and sweet).
Lots of leeks, and lettuce. Asparagus spears.
And a row of pumpkins, all of which he sells
on market day in town, his shoulders laden
on the way there, but on the way home, his purse.
Onions, mostly the red ones. Many chives.
Bitter watercress and some rocket plants
(rocket is said to be good for impotence).
        So he goes out to the garden and digs with his fingers
into the rich loam and finds four bulbs
of garlic, which he puts in his little bag.

Some parsley leaves, a little rue, coriander
that trembles on its frail stalk . . . These too
he takes inside, where he sits down near the fire
to peel the heavy outer skin from the garlic.
He calls to the maid who brings him his mortar and pestle
and in it he puts the peeled garlic pieces
and some of the various leaves. With a little water
and salt and a bit of the cheese he starts to grind
the mixture into a kind of juicy paste.
Around and around his muscular hand goes
until the ingredients give up their own flavors
to join in that of the combination, as many
different colors will blend into one dark hue.
The colors here, too, meld into a pale
green with flecks of dark and of milky white.
      There's a sharp tang, the kind you get when you slice
onions, and he has to blink away tears
or wipe his watering eyes with the back of his hand,
grumbling in discomfort as he does so.
      The mixture thickens. The pestle goes slower now,
as if it had taken on weight. In deliberate circles
he continues, however, and into the rich paste pours
some drops of olive oil and, to balance that,
some vinegar that he's put by for the purpose.
More mixing now and, when the mess has reached
its perfect consistency, he takes out the pestle
and with two fingers scrapes the sides of the mortar
to mold its contents into a ball of pesto
(sophisticates in Rome call it *moretum*).

And there it is. Scybale takes the bread,
which is ready now, out of its place in the hearth
and gives it to him. That, with the pesto, will be
lunch. He puts his gaiters on his legs,
grabs his hat, and goes out to yoke his bullocks
to drive them into the field to begin to plow.

THE GOOD MAN

Chaerephon, the Athenian poet, inquired
of the oracle at Delphi what men were wise
and honest. The woman on the tripod, inspired,
said to him, after one of her long sighs,

"Socrates. Perhaps." It is a tough
question, which is depressing. Of all mankind
living or dead, just one was good enough
for Apollo, after a pause, to bring to mind.

What is such a man like? Indifferent to
the opinions of the great unwashed, as well
as the attitudes of the rich and powerful few.
He's like a mollusk in his protective shell.

Or say that he is like a globe without
projections or declivities. He can
thus resist external assaults and flout
conventional ideas. He's his own man.

He lives an examined life and does not rest
at night until he has reviewed the way
he has behaved. Has he done his very best
at every challenge that he faced that day?

"Have I taken pity on the poor? Have I
grieved with the broken-hearted? Have I preferred
expediency's lures to honor? Why
have I been so thoughtless both in deed and word?"

Thus he catechizes himself and each
answer flagellates his maculate heart.
He knows his grasp was shorter than his reach
and promises—or prays—for a fresh start.

YES AND NO

These trivial monosyllables hold the world.
Take them away and there is only chaos
on the tongues of men. From them comes all our logic
at work or at play, exertion or quiet repose,
agreeing or disagreeing, whatever the subject.
In concord we echo each other and say, "Yes, yes,"
but then there's a flaw, a snag, and one says, "No!"
from which comes a sudden cool or a heating up
to the strife that brings us to court, or goes beyond that
to the circus, the theaters, taverns, the Senate itself.
Husbands and wives, parents and children learn
to use these words without letting them go
too far into nasty quarrels. In the schools we learn
that they are philosophers' tools, and for rhetoricians
the weapons they use in debates. "You will grant that it's light?"
"Yes." "Then it must be daytime." "But no, no!
Torches may give us light, or flashes of lightning.
If it is light, it need not be daylight."
And so they go on. Yes to this, but no
to what you insist that the first assent implies.
Do they squabble to find the truth? Or is it a game?
Men lose patience and bite their lips in a silent
rage beyond all words, even these two
syllables, the pivots of all our thinking.

BUDDING ROSES

On a springtime morning under a saffron-colored sky,
   night's biting chill was just giving way to a hint
of the warmth that was yet to come. I was walking a country path
   between well-tended plots and enjoying the crisp
tonic of fresh air. On the blades of grass I could see
   the white hoar-frost still clinging. On cabbage leaves
it had melted to crystal drops that agglomerated together.
. . . .
There were bushes with budding roses of the kind one finds at Paestum,
   dewy and gleaming in early morning light.
Here and there were those droplets, newborn but already drying
   in the first light of the sun. One supposed that the pink
touch of Aurora's progress stole its hue from these
   blushing rosebuds, although the converse seemed
plausible too—that the sky's tender tinge informed
   these opening buds and gave them their fresh color.
Venus, after all, is the queen of the morning and rules
   over these flowers as well, the tint, the moistness
clearly her own. Let her therefore take all the credit
   for the sky and the buds too, the freshness and fragrance
they share coming from her, the queen goddess of Paphos.
   It was just that critical moment when the buds were about
to split into equal segments their outer green containers.
   One's green calyx was closed; another's sepals
were about to separate and display the corolla's ruddy
   hints of what the blossom would soon be.
The next was already showing the spread of petals, within
   the cup of which were the saffron-yellow seeds.

But not far away on the same branch were overblown
          roses, the petals' array already going
or gone, and down on the grass their delicacy was fading.
          How swift is the ruin of beauty like this, how brusque,
budding, blooming, and dying all at once in a blur
          of being! I say the words that float on the air
and I watch as another petal lets go its hold and falls
          to carpet the green below with flashes of crimson.
I breathe the scent of the flowers, but every breath I take
          is all at once a birth and growth and death.
This is what Nature does, giving us mere glimpses
          she then snatches away, perhaps to mock us,
or is it to concentrate our ill-focused attention?
          In the case of a rose, a day is a whole lifetime
so that youth and age go hand in hand. The Morning Star
          sees a blossom born that, on her return
as the Evening Star, is already withered and dying.
          In a stern frame of mind I tell myself
that the blossom may die, but life springs back and renews
          the healthy bush. Is this enough to cheer me?
O maidens, gather your roses when you find them fresh,
          for they—and I fear you too—are already dying.

Text and display Garamond Premier Pro
Compositor BookMatters, Berkeley   *Printer and binder* Thomson-Shore, Inc.